contents

Key

- Number and Place value
- Addition and Subtraction
- Multiplication and Division
- Shape, Data and Measure
- Fractions and Decimals
- Mixed Operations

How to use this book

Read the instructions carefully before each set of questions.

The first page of each section will have a title telling you what the next few pages are about.

Sometimes a character will give you a tip.

Your teacher may tell you to GRAB something that might help you answer the questions.

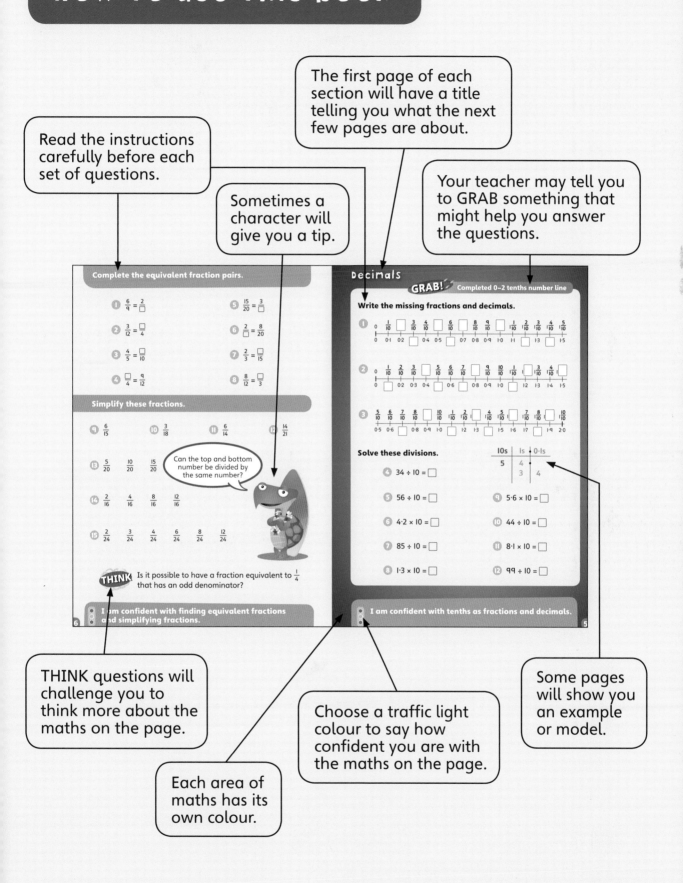

THINK questions will challenge you to think more about the maths on the page.

Each area of maths has its own colour.

Choose a traffic light colour to say how confident you are with the maths on the page.

Some pages will show you an example or model.

Bonds to multiples of 100

Find the missing numbers.

1 34 + ☐ = 100

2 ☐ + 68 = 200

3 200 − 105 = ☐

4 ☐ + 17 = 100

5 200 − ☐ = 77

6 135 + ☐ = 200

7 200 − ☐ = 144

8 100 − 51 = ☐

9 ☐ + 57 = 200

10 ☐ + 84 = 100

11 200 − 83 = ☐

12 200 − ☐ = 136

Write how much change from £1 you get if you pay:

13 56p

14 73p

15 42p

16 19p

Write how much change from £2 you get if you pay:

17 83p

18 £1·43

19 £1·64

20 32p

Write how much change from £5 you get if you pay:

21 44p

22 77p

23 £4·05

24 £4·26

I am confident with bonds to 100, 200 and 500.

1 $634 + \square = 700$

2 $\square + 78 = 400$

3 $800 - 49 = \square$

4 $\square + 27 = 600$

5 $400 - \square = 79$

6 $832 + \square = 900$

7 $600 - 564 = \square$

8 $633 + \square = 700$

9 $800 - \square = 744$

10 $700 - 631 = \square$

11 $\square + 57 = 600$

12 $\square + 614 = 700$

13 $900 - 823 = \square$

14 $700 - \square = 666$

15 $1000 - 981 = \square$

16 $800 - \square = 714$

17 Jim must drive 500 miles to Glasgow. By 5 o'clock he has driven 421 miles. How much further has he to go?

18 In a sale a TV that cost £400 is reduced by £73. How much does it cost now?

19 How much is the laptop in the sale?

 **THINK** Write your own word problem for the subtraction: $700 - 673$

I am confident with bonds to any multiple of 100.

Add or subtract to reach the next or previous 100

GRAB! **Landmarked number lines**

1 Copy this line. Fill in the missing jump values and complete the addition and subtraction to reach 200 and 300.

234

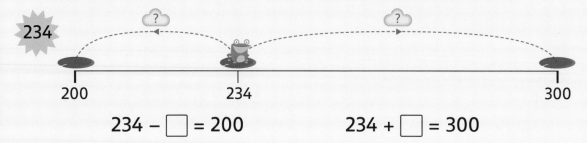

200	234	300

$234 - \square = 200$ $234 + \square = 300$

2 Copy and complete this line. Mark on 573 and draw the jumps. Fill in the missing jump values and complete the addition and subtraction to reach 500 and 600.

573

500	600

$573 - \square = 500$ $573 + \square = 600$

Draw number lines to help you complete these pairs of additions and subtractions.

3 $632 - \square = 600$ - - - - - - - - - - $632 + \square = 700$

4 $481 - \square = 400$ - - - - - - - - - - $481 + \square = 500$

5 $727 - \square = 700$ - - - - - - - - - - $727 + \square = 800$

6 $848 - \square = 800$ - - - - - - - - - - $848 + \square = 900$

7 $664 - \square = 600$ - - - - - - - - - - $664 + \square = 700$

8 $923 - \square = 900$ - - - - - - - - - - $923 + \square = 1000$

I am confident with adding to reach the next multiple of 100 and subtracting to reach the previous multiple of 100.

1. Copy this line. Fill in the missing jump values and complete the addition and subtraction to reach 6300 and 6400.

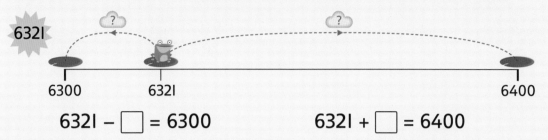

6321

6300   6321   6400

$6321 - \square = 6300$ $6321 + \square = 6400$

2. Copy and complete this line. Then use it to help you complete the addition and subtraction to reach 2500 and 2600.

2573

2500   2600

$2573 - \square = 2500$ $2573 + \square = 2600$

Draw lines and complete these additions and subtractions.

3. $7645 - \square = 7600$ ----------- $7645 + \square = 7700$

4. $6821 - \square = 6800$ ----------- $6821 + \square = 6900$

5. Copy this line. Fill in the missing jump values and complete the addition and subtraction to reach 7000 and 8000.

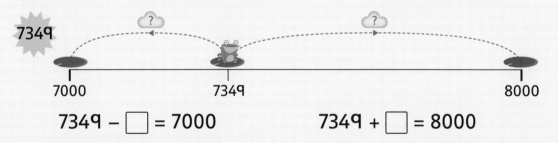

7349

7000   7349   8000

$7349 - \square = 7000$ $7349 + \square = 8000$

Draw lines and complete these additions and subtractions.

6. $8556 - \square = 8000$ ----------- $8556 + \square = 9000$

7. $4841 - \square = 4000$ ----------- $4841 + \square = 5000$

> **I am confident with adding to reach the next multiple of 100 or 1000 and subtracting to reach the previous multiple of 100 or 1000.**

Count up to find the difference

**Complete the subtraction to match the jotting.
Use similar jottings to answer the rest. You can use
either two or three jumps to help you.**

1   222 – 187 = ☐

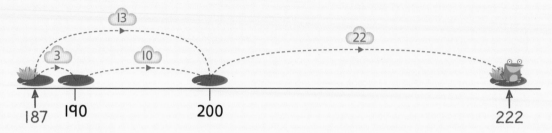

2   334 – 275 = ☐

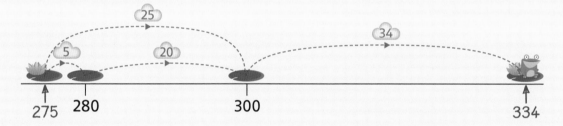

3   433 – 368 = ☐

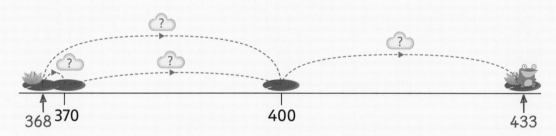

4   421 – 385 = ☐   **7**   431 – 377 = ☐

5   713 – 682 = ☐   **8**   542 – 485 = ☐

6   624 – 569 = ☐   **9**   533 – 479 = ☐

**I am confident with subtracting by counting up to
find the difference.**

Complete the subtraction to match the jotting. Use similar jottings to answer the rest. You can use either two or three jumps to help you answer.

GRAB! **Landmarked number lines**

1 343 − 287 = ☐

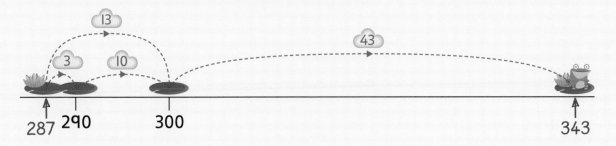

287 290   300   343

2 427 − 348 = ☐

348 350   400   427

3 658 − 574 = ☐

574 580   600   658

4 834 − 785 = ☐   **7** 971 − 884 = ☐

5 723 − 687 = ☐   **8** 772 − 645 = ☐

6 624 − 569 = ☐   **9** 563 − 429 = ☐

I am confident with subtracting by counting up to find the difference.

Adding several numbers

Find each total.

1 7 + 2 + 4 + 6 = ☐

2 5 + 7 + 6 + 3 = ☐

3 9 + 5 + 4 + 3 = ☐

4 50 + 30 + 60 + 20 = ☐

5 30 + 90 + 70 + 60 = ☐

6 40 + 20 + 80 + 60 = ☐

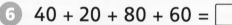

7 400 + 500 + 300 + 800 = ☐

8 700 + 200 + 400 + 500 = ☐

9 700 + 300 + 800 + 600 = ☐

○
○ **I am confident with adding four 1-, 2- and 3- digit**
○ **numbers.**

1

= 8 + 2 + 3 + 1 = ☐

80 + 20 + ☐0 + ☐0 = ☐

800 + ☐00 + ☐00 + ☐00 = ☐

2

= 4 + 5 + 8 + 6 = ☐

☐0 + ☐0 + ☐0 + ☐0 = ☐

☐00 + ☐00 + ☐00 + ☐00 = ☐

3

= 9 + 5 + 2 + 8 = ☐

☐0 + ☐0 + ☐0 + ☐0 = ☐

☐00 + ☐00 + ☐00 + ☐00 = ☐

 Write patterns of questions like those above that have the answers 18, 180 and 1800.

I am confident with adding four 1-, 2- and 3-digit numbers and spotting patterns in related additions.

1 score 25

3 + 4 + 4 + 3

3 + 6 + 3 + 7

2 score 19

8 + 3 + 4 + 9

3 score 14

6 + 7 + 3 + 9

4 score 170

30 + 10 + 60 + 50

40 + 60 + 50 + 60

5 score 210

20 + 30 + 60 + 60

6 score 180

60 + 30 + 30 + 60

7 score 2800

400 + 700 + 100 + 300

300 + 400 + 700 + 900

8 score 1500

900 + 100 + 900 + 900

9 score 2200

600 + 700 + 300 + 600

I am confident with adding four 1-, 2- and 3-digit numbers and spotting patterns in related additions.

4-digit numbers

Write these numbers in figures.

1. six thousand, two hundred and fifteen

2. four thousand and thirty-six

3. two thousand, six hundred and four

4. nine thousand and eleven

5. eight thousand and forty

6. one thousand and nine

Answer these questions.

7. $857 - 30 = \square$

8. $4276 + 500 = \square$

9. $8362 - 2000 = \square$

10. $9662 + 30 = \square$

11. $1639 + 200 = \square$

12. $6229 + 40 = \square$

13. $5537 - 300 = \square$

14. $2758 + 4000 = \square$

15. $9466 - 60 = \square$

16. $6558 - 6000 = \square$

 THINK A 4-digit number has the digits 4, 3, 0 and 0. Write all the possible numbers it could be in figures and words.

I am confident with place value in 4-digit numbers.

Write these numbers in figures.

1 nine thousand and twenty-four

2 six thousand, three hundred and two

3 seven thousand and eighty

4 two thousand and seven

5 eight thousand and sixteen

6 three thousand and thirty-nine

Answer these questions.

7 $9573 - 570 = \boxed{}$

8 $4284 - 4200 = \boxed{}$

9 $7362 - 302 = \boxed{}$

10 $8835 - 8005 = \boxed{}$

11 $5672 - 201 = \boxed{}$

12 $4223 + 410 = \boxed{}$

13 $9625 - 302 = \boxed{}$

14 $3278 + 4020 = \boxed{}$

15 $6946 + 2003 = \boxed{}$

16 $8494 - 370 = \boxed{}$

 A subtraction has the answer 2050. Write at least five different questions with that answer.

Write these pairs of numbers with the correct > or < sign between them.

① 326   472

② 582   594

③ 1347   872

④ 949   1408

⑤ 3421   2167

⑥ 4892   9173

Answer these questions.

⑦ The number is 354. Write the number that is:
I more   10 more
I less   10 less

⑧ The number is 4263. Write the number that is:
I more   10 more
I less   10 less

⑨ The number is 500. Write the number that is:
I more   10 more
I less   10 less

⑩ The number is 2450. Write the number that is:
I more   10 more
I less   10 less

THINK I think of a 4-digit number. I add 10 to it, then subtract 100 and finally add 1. The answer is 4294. What was the number?

I am confident with place value and ordering of 4-digit numbers.

15

Write these pairs of numbers with the correct > or < sign between them.

1. 379   973
2. 707   907
3. 7484   7326

4. 4519   4527
5. 2020   2002
6. 4092   9106

Answer these questions.

7. The number is 6325. Write the number that is:

1 more	10 more
1 less	10 less

8. The number is 1743. Write the number that is:

1 more	10 more
1 less	10 less

9. The number is 4927. Write the number that is:

1 more	10 more
1 less	10 less

10. The number is 5205. Write the number that is:

1 more	10 more
1 less	10 less

11. The number is 7690. Write the number that is:

1 more	10 more
1 less	10 less

○ **I am confident with place value and ordering of**
○ **4-digit numbers.**
○
○

16

Write these pairs of numbers with the correct > or < sign between them.

1. 9462   9426

2. 7587   7785

3. 3898   3889

4. 4254   4245

5. 6457   6547

6. 4654   4565

Write >, < or = between each pair.

7. 4069   3469 + 900

8. 2174   2614 – 300

9. 4552 + 20   4572

10. 6794   6715 + 80

11. 5684   6049 – 400

12. 4612 + 30   4912 – 300

13. 5868 – 200   5026 + 800

14. 3715 + 90   4016 – 200

 **THINK**   Write two more of your own.

I am confident with place value and ordering of 4-digit numbers.

Write the missing tag numbers.

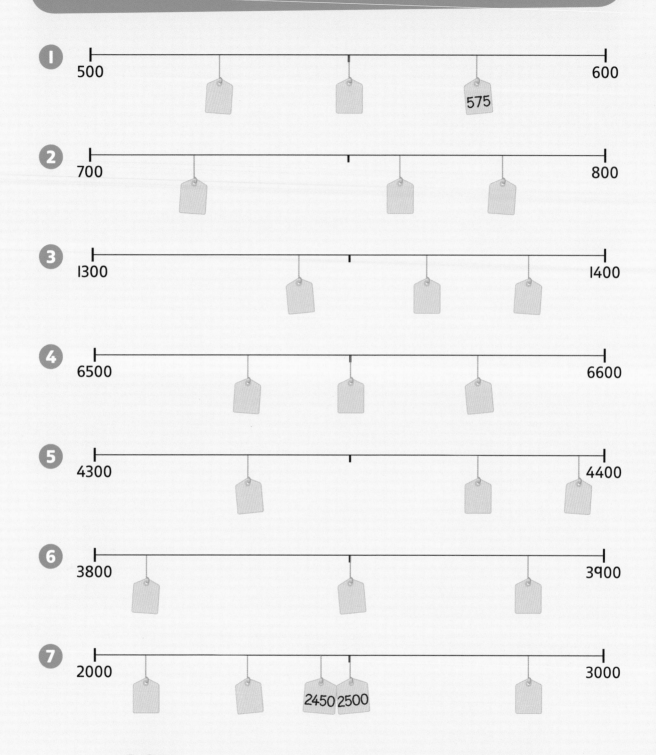

1 500 — 575 — 600

2 700 — 800

3 1300 — 1400

4 6500 — 6600

5 4300 — 4400

6 3800 — 3900

7 2000 — 2450 2500 — 3000

THINK Draw a 1000 to 2000 number line of your own and mark on some numbers.

I am confident with placing 4-digit numbers on a number line.

18

Write the missing tag numbers.

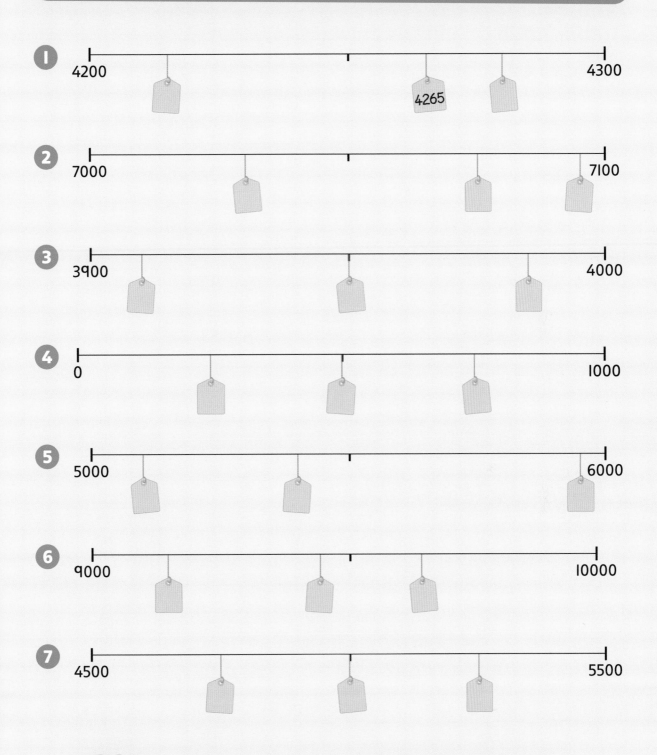

1 4200 ___ 4265 ___ 4300

2 7000 ___ ___ ___ 7100

3 3900 ___ ___ ___ 4000

4 0 ___ ___ ___ 1000

5 5000 ___ ___ ___ 6000

6 9000 ___ ___ ___ 10000

7 4500 ___ ___ ___ 5500

THINK Draw a line from 2500 to 3500. Mark on the three numbers 2600, 3000 and 3150.

I am confident with placing 4-digit numbers on a number line.

Add these numbers.

1. $42 + 23 = \square$
2. $26 + 41 = \square$
3. $55 + 24 = \square$
4. $33 + 46 = \square$
5. $36 + 45 = \square$
6. $28 + 33 = \square$
7. $38 + 44 = \square$
8. $63 + 29 = \square$

9. $45 + 38 = \square$
10. $63 + 72 = \square$
11. $44 + 74 = \square$
12. $83 + 54 = \square$
13. $75 + 82 = \square$
14. $56 + 57 = \square$
15. $76 + 44 = \square$
16. $85 + 68 = \square$

Answer these questions.

17. There are 36 cars parked on level 1 and 47 cars parked on level 2. How many cars are there altogether?

18. Jane is 78 cm tall. Chloe is 28 cm taller than Jane. How tall is Chloe?

THINK Write three additions with an answer of 64. Have you got the same three as the person sitting next to you?

I am confident with adding two 2-digit numbers.

Find the totals.

1. 42 + 23 + 18 = ☐
2. 35 + 26 + 31 = ☐
3. 36 + 25 + 24 = ☐
4. 33 + 26 + 28 = ☐
5. 26 + 48 + 19 = ☐
6. 28 + 37 + 28 = ☐

7. 32 + 44 + 51 = ☐
8. 63 + 72 + 33 = ☐
9. 65 + 44 + 74 = ☐
10. 67 + 83 + 54 = ☐
11. 75 + 56 + 82 = ☐
12. 94 + 68 + 57 = ☐

Add these numbers.

13. 625 + 36 = ☐
14. 356 + 27 = ☐
15. 485 + 21 = ☐
16. 526 + 82 = ☐

17. 363 + 75 = ☐
18. 875 + 38 = ☐
19. 544 + 77 = ☐
20. 748 + 65 = ☐

 A 2-digit number and a 3-digit number have the same total as three 2-digit numbers.

What could the numbers be?

I am confident with adding 2-digit and 3-digit numbers.

21

Subtracting 2-digit and 3-digit numbers

Answer each subtraction using the method shown.

Count up   **Take away**

1 82 – 47 = ☐

2 91 – 68 = ☐

3 73 – 56 = ☐

4 84 – 67 = ☐

5 92 – 55 = ☐

6 63 – 48 = ☐

7 95 – 21 = ☐

8 86 – 32 = ☐

9 97 – 23 = ☐

10 89 – 22 = ☐

11 98 – 34 = ☐

12 85 – 21 = ☐

Choose a method to answer each of these.

13 96 – 11 = ☐

14 82 – 76 = ☐

15 93 – 68 = ☐

16 85 – 13 = ☐

17 96 – 22 = ☐

18 81 – 66 = ☐

○
○   **I am confident with choosing the best subtraction**
○   **method to use.**

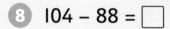

You could count up using Frog or take away!

1. 93 – 58 = ☐

2. 158 – 23 = ☐

3. 83 – 67 = ☐

4. 88 – 31 = ☐

5. 195 – 32 = ☐

6. 123 – 94 = ☐

7. 134 – 23 = ☐

8. 104 – 88 = ☐

9. 137 – 82 = ☐

10. 155 – 63 = ☐

11. 128 – 74 = ☐

12. 126 – 35 = ☐

13. 175 – 89 = ☐

14. 166 – 72 = ☐

 **THINK** Did you work out questions 13 and 14 in the same way as your partner? If not, discuss why.

I am confident with choosing the best subtraction method to use.

Take away?

1. 143 − 87 = ☐

2. 283 − 31 = ☐

3. 583 − 62 = ☐

4. 186 − 34 = ☐

5. 195 − 74 = ☐

6. 123 − 94 = ☐

7. 104 − 63 = ☐

8. 605 − 22 = ☐

9. 137 − 88 = ☐

10. 767 − 82 = ☐

11. 142 − 60 = ☐

12. 126 − 69 = ☐

13. 371 − 74 = ☐

14. 156 − 85 = ☐

15. 112 − 67 = ☐

16. 563 − 72 = ☐

THINK A 2-digit number has identical digits. It is subtracted from 135. What are the possible answers?

The 6 times-table

Write the missing number for each calculation.

1. $2 \times 6 = \boxed{}$

2. $18 \div 6 = \boxed{}$

3. $\boxed{} \times 6 = 30$

4. $60 \div 6 = \boxed{}$

5. $\boxed{} \times 6 = 24$

6. $11 \times 6 = \boxed{}$

7. $\boxed{} \times 6 = 36$

8. $5 \times 6 = \boxed{}$

9. $6 \div 6 = \boxed{}$

10. $42 \div 6 = \boxed{}$

11. $\boxed{} \div 6 = 8$

12. $6 \times 6 = \boxed{}$

13. $\boxed{} \div 6 = 9$

14. $72 \div 6 = \boxed{}$

15. $7 \times 6 = \boxed{}$

16. $0 \times 6 = \boxed{}$

Answer these questions.

17. How much for 3 DVDs?

Climbing — Space DVD — OUTDOOR DVD — Tennis — Coast

DVDs £6 EACH

18. How many eggs in total?

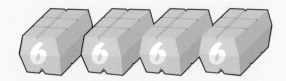

19. Jack saves £6 each week. How many weeks must he save to afford a model car that costs £48?

20. Rani runs 6 km each day. How far does she run in one week (7 days)?

○ **I am confident with the 6 times-table.**
○
○

Write each missing number.

1. $5 \times 6 = \square$

2. $\square \div 6 = 6$

3. $\square \times 6 = 6$

4. $66 \div 6 = \square$

5. $12 \times 6 = \square$

6. $0 \div 6 = \square$

7. $7 \times 6 = \square$

8. $\square \div 6 = 9$

9. $\square \div 6 = 8$

10. $3 \times 6 = \square$

11. $\square \div 6 = 4$

12. $72 \div 6 = \square$

Answer these problems.

13. Lin gets £6 each week for pocket money. After how many weeks will she have £54?

14. Dan has some building blocks. Each is 6 cm tall. How tall is a tower of 12 of the blocks?

Use facts you know to answer the questions.

15. Use 7×6 to answer $\text{------} 14 \times 6 = \square$

16. Use 12×6 to answer $\text{------} 24 \times 6 = \square$

17. Use 9×6 to answer $\text{------} 27 \times 6 = \square$

THINK Use other facts from the 6 times-table. Write some related facts in the same way.

● I am confident with the 6 times-table.

The 9 times-table

1 Write these multiples of 9:

$2 \times 9 = \square$ $5 \times 9 = \square$ $8 \times 9 = \square$

$3 \times 9 = \square$ $6 \times 9 = \square$ $9 \times 9 = \square$

$4 \times 9 = \square$ $7 \times 9 = \square$ $10 \times 9 = \square$

2 Add up the digits of each answer, starting with 1 + 8. What do you notice?

3 Answer $11 \times 9 = \square$ and add up the digits of the answer. If the number has 2 digits, add them together. What do you get?

4 The number 378 is a multiple of 9.

| 378 | | 3 + 7 + 8 = 18 | ⟶ | 1 + 8 = 9 |

Write how you can tell it is a multiple of 9.

Add the digits of each number and say whether it is a multiple of 9.

$1 + 1 + 7 = \square$

5 | 117 |

6 | 603 |

7 | 224 |

8 | 882 |

9 | 658 |

10 | 909 |

THINK   Write a really big number that is a multiple of 9.

○
○ **I am confident with the 9 times-table and**
○ **recognising multiples of 9.**

Write each missing number.

1. $5 \times 9 = \square$
2. $\square \div 9 = 6$
3. $\square \times 9 = 9$
4. $18 \div 9 = \square$
5. $12 \times 9 = \square$

6. $7 \times 9 = \square$
7. $\square \div 9 = 9$
8. $\square \div 9 = 8$
9. $3 \times 9 = \square$
10. $\square \div 9 = 4$

Answer these questions.

11. Write the multiples of 9 from 9 to 108. Add the digits of each answer. What do you notice?

12. The numbers 459 and 999 are multiples of 9.

| 459 | $4 + 5 + 9 = 18$ | $\longrightarrow$ | $1 + 8 = 9$ |
| 999 | $9 + 9 + 9 = 27$ | $\longrightarrow$ | $2 + 7 = 9$ |

Write all the multiples of 9 that are in the cloud below.

64
118   901
222   36   27   423
18   936   77   909   45
108   99   117   100   135

13. Write all the multiples of 9 between 110 and 150.

14. Write all the multiples of 9 between 700 and 750.

I am confident with the 9 times-table and recognising multiples of 9.

Multiplying 2-digit numbers by a 1-digit number

Copy and complete:

GRAB! **Counting sticks**

1
| 0 | 5 | ☐ | ☐ | ☐ | ☐ | ☐ | ☐ | ☐ | 45 | ☐ |

| 0 | 50 | 100 | 150 | ☐ | ☐ | ☐ | 350 | ☐ | ☐ | 500 |

Answer each pair of questions.

2 $6 \times 2 = \square$
    $6 \times 20 = \square$

3 $2 \times 6 = \square$
    $2 \times 60 = \square$

4 $5 \times 5 = \square$
    $5 \times 50 = \square$

5 $6 \times 4 = \square$
    $6 \times 40 = \square$

6 $4 \times 3 = \square$
    $4 \times 30 = \square$

7 $7 \times 3 = \square$
    $7 \times 30 = \square$

8 $5 \times 4 = \square$
    $5 \times 40 = \square$

9 $3 \times 9 = \square$
    $3 \times 90 = \square$

10 $6 \times 6 = \square$
     $6 \times 60 = \square$

11 $7 \times 9 = \square$
     $7 \times 90 = \square$

○
○ **I am confident with multiplying multiples of 10 by**
○ **1-digit numbers.**

Use the grid method or partitioning to multiply these numbers.

1. $42 \times 3 = \square$
2. $13 \times 8 = \square$
3. $4 \times 23 = \square$
4. $67 \times 2 = \square$
5. $6 \times 22 = \square$
6. $14 \times 9 = \square$
7. $6 \times 34 = \square$

8. $26 \times 8 = \square$
9. $9 \times 47 = \square$
10. $86 \times 5 = \square$
11. $4 \times 68 = \square$
12. $96 \times 4 = \square$
13. $8 \times 77 = \square$
14. $87 \times 9 = \square$

Solve these problems.

15. A lorry delivers 6 crates of cola. There are 24 bottles in each crate. How many bottles are there?

16. Each chocolate bar costs 67p. How much do 3 bars cost?

17. Cherry tomatoes weigh 9 g each. How much do 27 of them weigh?

18. Each class in Hawsker School has 28 pupils. The school has 8 classes. How many pupils are there in the school?

 **THINK**   What could the missing digits be?

$$5\,\square \times 5 = \square\,\square\,5$$

Use the grid method or partitioning to multiply these numbers. Estimate each answer first.

1   87 × 3 = ☐

2   46 × 8 = ☐

3   4 × 77 = ☐

4   67 × 9 = ☐

5   8 × 69 = ☐

6   48 × 9 = ☐

7   84 × 8 = ☐

8   9 × 69 = ☐

9   73 × 6 = ☐

10   9 × 68 = ☐

11   78 × 6 = ☐

12   8 × 87 = ☐

Solve these problems.

13   Biscuits come in packs of 8. How many biscuits are there in 36 packs?

14   Each orange costs 58p. How much do 9 oranges cost?

15   An egg-cup can hold 64 ml of water. Mrs Fuller pours 7 egg-cups full of water into a bottle. How many millilitres of water did she put into the bottle?

 **THINK**   Copy and complete this grid method calculation.

×		
	160	12	=

I am confident with multiplying 2-digit numbers by 1-digit numbers.

31

Finding unit fractions of amounts

Find these fractions.

1. $\frac{1}{3}$ of 24 = ☐

2. $\frac{1}{2}$ of 52 = ☐

3. $\frac{1}{10}$ of 40 = ☐

4. $\frac{1}{5}$ of 35 = ☐

5. $\frac{1}{4}$ of 48 = ☐

6. $\frac{1}{3}$ of 27 = ☐

7. $\frac{1}{5}$ of 60 = ☐

8. $\frac{1}{8}$ of 32 = ☐

9. $\frac{1}{9}$ of 63 = ☐

10. $\frac{1}{6}$ of 36 = ☐

11. $\frac{1}{9}$ of 99 = ☐

12. $\frac{1}{8}$ of 56 = ☐

13. Obi had £500. He gave $\frac{1}{10}$ of this money to charity. How much did he give?

Copy and complete, writing one of these signs: >, < or = between each pair.

14. $\frac{1}{3}$ of 9 $\frac{1}{4}$ of 8

15. $\frac{1}{3}$ of 18 $\frac{1}{4}$ of 24

16. $\frac{1}{2}$ of 24 $\frac{1}{5}$ of 55

17. $\frac{1}{10}$ of 60 $\frac{1}{6}$ of 54

 THINK   Make up two more of your own like this.

⊙ **I am confident with finding unit fractions of amounts.**

Find these fractions.

1. $\frac{1}{6}$ of 42 = ☐

2. $\frac{1}{8}$ of 48 = ☐

3. $\frac{1}{9}$ of 36 = ☐

4. $\frac{1}{8}$ of 88 = ☐

5. $\frac{1}{4}$ of 32 = ☐

6. $\frac{1}{3}$ of 36 = ☐

7. $\frac{1}{9}$ of 54 = ☐

8. $\frac{1}{8}$ of 64 = ☐

9. $\frac{1}{6}$ of 72 = ☐

10. $\frac{1}{4}$ of 400 = ☐

11. $\frac{1}{9}$ of 108 = ☐

12. $\frac{1}{8}$ of 96 = ☐

Copy and complete the patterns.

> The first answer helps with the second answer in each pair.

13. $\frac{1}{5}$ of 60 = ☐

    $\frac{2}{5}$ of 60 = ☐

14. $\frac{1}{3}$ of 21 = ☐

    $\frac{2}{3}$ of 21 = ☐

15. $\frac{1}{8}$ of 64 = ☐

    $\frac{3}{8}$ of 64 = ☐

16. $\frac{1}{9}$ of 81 = ☐

    $\frac{5}{9}$ of 81 = ☐

 **THINK** Make up some similar patterns of your own.

○
○ **I am confident with finding unit and non-unit**
○ **fractions of amounts.**

Telling the time to the minute

Draw hands onto analogue clock faces to show these times.

1 `6:05`

2 `8:22`

3 `4:19`

4 `11:08`

5 `10:12`

6 `1:42`

7 `9:54`

8 `7:37`

9 `12:48`

Draw each of these as a digital time.

10

11

12

13

14

15

16 Choose two of the analogue times and write them in words.

 THINK Look at clock 7. What will the time be in 7 minutes?

○
○ **I am confident with telling and writing analogue**
○ **and digital times.**

Write how many minutes until the next o'clock time and what time that will be.

1  8:02

4  12:27

7 9:16

2  4:36

5 11:32

8 8:39

3  8:19

6 2:43

9 12:51

Do the same for these times.

10

12

14

11

13

15

THINK

Continue this pattern and write each as a digital time.

one minute to 1, two minutes to 2, three minutes to 3, four minutes to 4...up to twelve minutes to 12.

I am confident with telling the time and working out the next o'clock time.

How long is each programme?

Smart Art shows from 7:45 to 8:30.

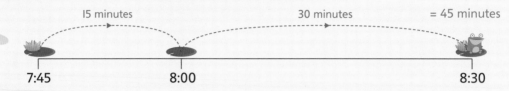

15 minutes   30 minutes   = 45 minutes

7:45   8:00   8:30

1   *Tea with Me* shows from 3:40 to 4:20.

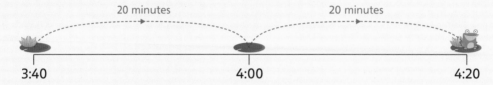

20 minutes   20 minutes

3:40   4:00   4:20

2   *Chatterbox* shows from 2:50 to 3:25.

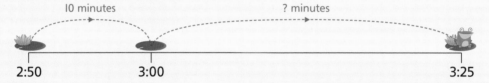

10 minutes   ? minutes

2:50   3:00   3:25

3   *Sport News* shows from 10:30 to 11:10.

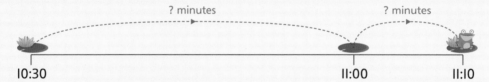

? minutes   ? minutes

10:30   11:00   11:10

4   *Funny Facts* shows from 12:40 to 1:35.

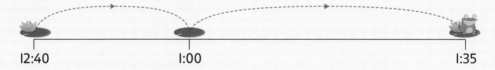

12:40   1:00   1:35

5   *Cassie* shows from 7:45 to 8:25.

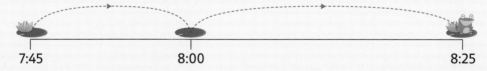

7:45   8:00   8:25

6   *Scary Stan* shows from 3:35 to 4:15.

I am confident with working out time intervals within 1 hour.

On TV Today

Mishmash	2:50
Wisher's Well	3:35
The Mystery of Coleman Brook	4:15
Funny Faces	4:40
Sandy and Scott	5:25
Emergency Call-out	6:05
Baker's Chase	6:45
Time Travellers	7:35
Evening News	8:20
The Back-beat Band	9:05

How long is each programme?

Mishmash

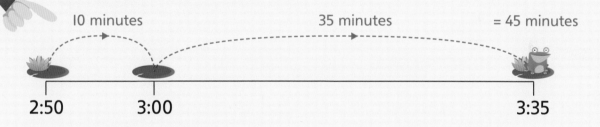

10 minutes   35 minutes   = 45 minutes

2:50   3:00   3:35

1 *Wisher's Well*   4 *Baker's Chase*

2 *Funny Faces*   5 *Time Travellers*

3 *Sandy and Scott*   6 *Evening News*

THINK A programme lasts 40 minutes. What time could it have started and finished?

I am confident with working out time intervals within 1 hour.

Train Timetable				
Hawkser	7:55 am	9:45 am	12:05 pm	3:25 pm
Scarby	8:45 am	10:35 am	12:50 pm	4:20 pm
Elton	9:25 am	11:15 am	1:30 pm	4:55 pm
Ashby	10:10 am	11:55 am	2:15 pm	5:30 pm

Use the timetable to help you answer the questions.

How long does the first train take to travel:

1. from Hawsker to Scarby?

4. from Hawsker to Elton?

2. from Scarby to Elton?

5. from Scarby to Ashby?

3. from Elton to Ashby?

6. from Hawsker to Ashby?

7. Sam is at Scarby at 9 o'clock in the morning. How long does she have to wait to get a train to Elton?

8. Jane needs to be in Ashby by 2 o'clock in the afternoon. What time should she catch the train from Elton?

9. Jack leaves Hawsker at five to eight in the morning and gets off at Scarby. Four hours and five minutes later he gets on another train to go to Elton. When does he reach Elton?

 **THINK** Which train takes the longest time to travel from Hawsker to Ashby?

I am confident with working out time intervals and reading timetables.

Centimetres and millimetres

Measure each line. Give each length in two ways, for example, 4 cm 6 mm and 4·6 cm.

1 _____

2 _____

3 _____

4 _____

5 _____

6 _____

7

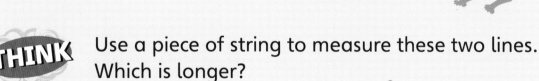

Draw lines of:

8 9·5 cm

9 4 cm 8 mm

10 12 cm 6 mm

11 7·2 cm

12 5 cm 8 mm

13 10·7 cm

THINK Use a piece of string to measure these two lines. Which is longer?

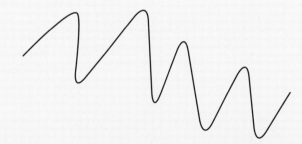

I am confident with measuring in centimetres and millimetres and I understand the relationship between the two.

Copy and convert these lengths.

1. 3 cm = ☐ mm

2. ☐ cm = 40 mm

3. 6 cm 4 mm = ☐ mm

4. 9 cm 3 mm = ☐ mm

5. ☐ cm ☐ mm = 39 mm

6. 7·2 cm = ☐ mm

7. ☐·☐ cm = 39 mm

8. 10 cm 4 mm = ☐ mm

9. ☐ cm = 600 mm

10. ☐·☐ cm = 124 mm

11. ☐ cm ☐ mm = 203 mm

12. 10·2 cm = ☐ mm

13. 19·4 cm = ☐ cm ☐ mm

14. 23 cm 2 mm = ☐·☐ cm

15. 20 cm 6 mm = ☐·☐ cm

16. 28·9 cm = ☐ cm ☐ mm

17. 16 cm 1 mm = ☐·☐ cm

18. 25·3 cm = ☐ cm ☐ mm

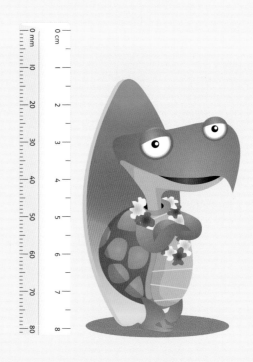

 **THINK** Write these lengths in order, starting with the smallest.

240 mm   23 cm 2 mm   2·5 cm   22·9 cm   30 mm

I am confident with converting between centimetres and millimetres.

Metres, centimetres and millimetres

Answer these length questions.

 Which of these animals could measure 123 cm in length?

a   b    c

② Which of these could measure 2 m 15 cm in length?

a    b    c

③ Which of these could measure 50 mm in length?

a    b    c

④ Which of these could measure 34 cm 2 mm in length?

a    b   c

THINK   Make up several puzzles of your own like these.

 **I am confident with estimating measurements in metres, centimetres and millimetres.**

482 + 64 =

	400	80	2		
+		60	4		
	400	140	6	=	546

Use this method to do these additions.

① 273 + 54 = ☐

② 645 + 38 = ☐

③ 772 + 83 = ☐

④ 326 + 45 = ☐

327 + 254 =

	300	20	7		
+	200	50	4		
	500	70	11	=	581

⑤ 482 + 264 = ☐

⑥ 354 + 185 = ☐

⑦ 634 + 238 = ☐

⑧ 381 + 357 = ☐

THINK Write an addition question that has an answer between 830 and 870.

I am confident with adding 2- and 3-digit numbers using the expanded method.

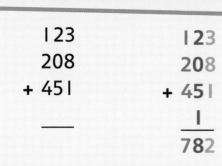

```
  123            123
  208            208
+ 451          + 451
 ____            1
                ___
                782
```

① 181
       312
     + 425
     ____

② 217
       444
     + 135
     ____

③ 363
       342
     + 283
     ____

④ 282
       162
     + 474
     ____

⑤ 554
       162
     + 245
     ____

⑥ 661
       128
     + 165
     ____

⑦ 483
       312
     + 412
     ____

⑧ 566
       303
     + 625
     ____

⑨ 373
       114
     + 413
     ____

⑩ 817
       336
     + 327
     ____

⑪ 784
       552
     + 527
     ____

⑫ 868
       616
     + 917
     ____

THINK Answer these and explain what patterns you notice.

```
  123            456            789
+ 987          + 654          + 321
 ____            ____           ____
```

I am confident with adding 3-digit numbers using column addition.

① Choose a number from each set and find the total.
Do this six times.

Set 1	Set 2	Set 3
384	255	473
583	841	265
494	809	792
835	352	407

Find the total for each addition.

②
```
  284
  413
+ 361
─────
```

⑤
```
  534
  832
+ 935
─────
```

⑧
```
  978
  165
+ 477
─────
```

③
```
  573
  656
+ 573
─────
```

⑥
```
  364
  188
+ 385
─────
```

⑨
```
  725
  833
+ 927
─────
```

④
```
  730
  687
+ 356
─────
```

⑦
```
  368
  319
+ 317
─────
```

⑩
```
  123
  456
+ 789
─────
```

THINK Find the totals of these and describe the patterns.

1234 + 4321   2345 + 5432   3456 + 6543

4567 + 7654   5678 + 8765   6789 + 9876

I am confident with adding 3-digit numbers using column addition.

44

Expanded column subtraction

GRAB! **Base 10 equipment**

```
              700   140
   849        800    40    9
 – 584     –  500    80    4
              200    60    5  =  265
```

Use this method to answer these subtractions.

1　726　　　　700　　20　　6
　　– 392　　　– 300　　90　　2

2　964　　　　900　　60　　4
　　– 283　　　– 200　　80　　3

3　987　　　**6**　554　　　**9**　776
　– 565　　　　　– 363　　　　　– 194

4　573　　　**7**　376　　　**10**　803
　– 381　　　　　– 263　　　　　– 662

5　417　　　**8**　829　　　**11**　678
　– 265　　　　　– 567　　　　　– 485

○
○ **I am confident with column subtraction of 3-digit**
○ **numbers using the expanded method.**

45

```
                    700   100
         809        800    0    9
       − 383      − 300    80   3
                    400    20   6   = 426
```

1 938
     − 674

2 816
     − 465

3 708
     − 486

4 825
     − 354

5 809
     − 366

6 914
     − 584

7 338
     − 265

8 759
     − 567

9 978
     − 884

10 783
      − 344

11 881
      − 667

12 893
      − 485

Write a subtraction that needs you to move a 10 into the 1s column instead of moving a 100 into the 10s column. Try out your subtraction on a partner. Can your partner solve it?

I am confident with column subtraction of 3-digit numbers using the expanded method.

Answer these using an expanded method of subtraction.

1   827
       − 563
       ‾‾‾‾‾

2   992
       − 465
       ‾‾‾‾‾

3   807
       − 392
       ‾‾‾‾‾

4   775
       − 359
       ‾‾‾‾‾

5   874
       − 565
       ‾‾‾‾‾

6   818
       − 687
       ‾‾‾‾‾

7   980
       − 451
       ‾‾‾‾‾

8   683
       − 277
       ‾‾‾‾‾

9   876
       − 384
       ‾‾‾‾‾

10 673
       − 234
       ‾‾‾‾‾

11 885
       − 769
       ‾‾‾‾‾

12 793
       − 287
       ‾‾‾‾‾

13

How much does the TV cost now then?

£849
£849 Reduced by £285
£849 Reduced by £285

14

DAILY NEWS
It is 541 m tall.

The Eiffel Tower is 217 metres shorter than that!

How tall is the Eiffel Tower?

I am confident with column subtraction of 3-digit numbers using the expanded method.

GRAB! Base 10 equipment

		60	13		
673	600	~~70~~	~~3~~		
− 348	− 300	40	8		
	300	20	5	=	325

		600	130			
737		~~700~~	~~30~~	7		
− 453	−	400	50	3		
		200	80	4	=	284

1 726   700 **20** 6
  − 392   − 300 **90** 2

2 964   900 **60** 4
  − 283   − 200 **80** 3

3 825   **5** 628   **7** 776
  − 595   − 385   − 268

4 368   **6** 894   **8** 806
  − 129   − 769   − 194

 **THINK** Choose three of your subtractions to check using Frog.

I am confident with column subtraction of
3-digit numbers using the expanded method.

Doubling 3-digit numbers

Double 324 is 648.

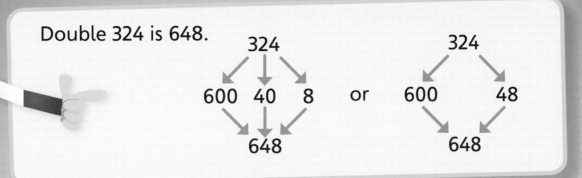

Or

Double these numbers.

1. 123
2. 421
3. 314
4. 234
5. 136
6. 248
7. 319

8. 237
9. 361
10. 482
11. 154
12. 293
13. 478
14. 396

 **THINK** Make as many different 3-digit numbers as you can using the digits 2, 4 and 7. Put the numbers in order and double each of the numbers.

○
○ **I am confident with doubling 3-digit numbers.**
○

Double these numbers.

1 126

2 473

3 328

4 164

5 413

6 249

7 375

8 347

9 253

10 466

11 268

12 387

13 489

14 442

15 184

16 277

17 356

18 843

19 738

20 926

THINK Find which numbers have been doubled.

☐

800   46

846

☐

600   74

674

• **I am confident with doubling 3-digit numbers.**

50

Halving 3-digit even numbers

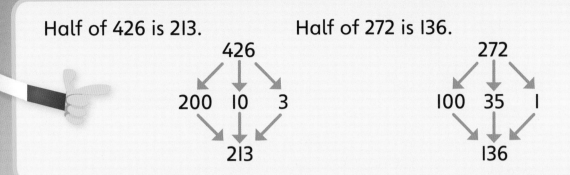

Half of 426 is 213.

```
        426
      ↙  ↓  ↘
   200   10   3
      ↘  ↓  ↙
        213
```

Half of 272 is 136.

```
        272
      ↙  ↓  ↘
   100   35   1
      ↘  ↓  ↙
        136
```

Halve these numbers.

1 84

2 46

3 446

4 824

5 288

6 264

7 74

8 278

9 56

10 652

11 342

12 566

13 A TV that cost £296 is now half price. How much is it now?

 **THINK** Jai thought of a number and halved it to get an answer of 231. What was the number?

○○○ **I am confident with halving 3-digit even numbers.**

Halve these numbers.

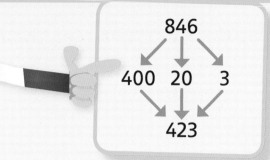

846

400 20 3

423

1 828

2 662

3 456

4 278

5 692

6 874

7 746

8 924

9 386

10 568

11 976

12 758

13 394

Solve these problems.

14 Hannah drives from home to York and back. The total distance driven was 326 km. How far from York is her home?

15 These items are being put into a sale. Find half price for each item.

a £3·00

b £4·20

c £5·68

d £2·76 *Magazine*

e £9·84

f £3·72

I am confident with halving 3-digit even numbers.

Unit fractions and equivalence

Copy these pairs of fractions and write > or < between them.

1. $\dfrac{1}{5}$ $\dfrac{1}{7}$

2. $\dfrac{1}{9}$ $\dfrac{1}{4}$

3. $\dfrac{1}{3}$ $\dfrac{1}{6}$

4. $\dfrac{1}{10}$ $\dfrac{1}{9}$

5. $\dfrac{1}{10}$ $\dfrac{1}{3}$

6. $\dfrac{1}{4}$ $\dfrac{1}{5}$

7. $\dfrac{1}{7}$ $\dfrac{1}{9}$

8. $\dfrac{1}{5}$ $\dfrac{1}{8}$

What fraction of each shape is shaded?

9.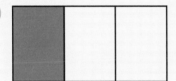

12.

15.

10.

13.

16.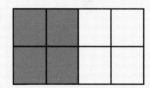

11.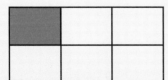

14.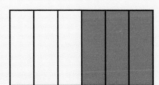

17.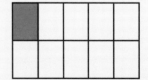

THINK  Can you write any of the fractions above using smaller numbers?

I am confident with ordering unit fractions and recognising fractions of a shape.

Copy these pairs of fractions and write > or < between them.

$$\frac{2}{3} > \frac{3}{5}$$

1 $\frac{1}{6}$ $\frac{1}{9}$

2 $\frac{1}{10}$ $\frac{1}{12}$

3 $\frac{1}{5}$ $\frac{1}{12}$

4 $\frac{1}{10}$ $\frac{1}{8}$

5 $\frac{2}{5}$ $\frac{7}{8}$

6 $\frac{3}{4}$ $\frac{7}{7}$

7 $\frac{2}{7}$ $\frac{5}{8}$

8 $\frac{4}{7}$ $\frac{3}{9}$

What fraction of each shape is shaded?

9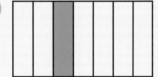

10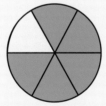

11

12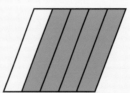

13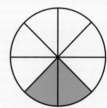

14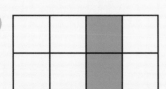

15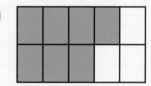

16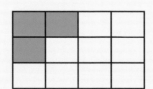

17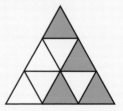

THINK   Can you write any of the fractions above using smaller numbers?

○
○   **I am confident with ordering unit and non-unit**
○   **fractions and recognising fractions of a shape.**

Use the fraction wall to help you with the questions below.

1 Whole									
$\frac{1}{2}$					$\frac{1}{2}$				
$\frac{1}{3}$			$\frac{1}{3}$			$\frac{1}{3}$			
$\frac{1}{4}$		$\frac{1}{4}$		$\frac{1}{4}$			$\frac{1}{4}$		
$\frac{1}{5}$		$\frac{1}{5}$		$\frac{1}{5}$		$\frac{1}{5}$		$\frac{1}{5}$	
$\frac{1}{6}$	$\frac{1}{6}$		$\frac{1}{6}$		$\frac{1}{6}$		$\frac{1}{6}$		$\frac{1}{6}$
$\frac{1}{7}$	$\frac{1}{7}$	$\frac{1}{7}$		$\frac{1}{7}$		$\frac{1}{7}$		$\frac{1}{7}$	$\frac{1}{7}$
$\frac{1}{8}$	$\frac{1}{8}$	$\frac{1}{8}$	$\frac{1}{8}$	$\frac{1}{8}$	$\frac{1}{8}$	$\frac{1}{8}$		$\frac{1}{8}$	
$\frac{1}{9}$	$\frac{1}{9}$	$\frac{1}{9}$	$\frac{1}{9}$	$\frac{1}{9}$	$\frac{1}{9}$	$\frac{1}{9}$	$\frac{1}{9}$	$\frac{1}{9}$	
$\frac{1}{10}$	$\frac{1}{10}$	$\frac{1}{10}$	$\frac{1}{10}$	$\frac{1}{10}$	$\frac{1}{10}$	$\frac{1}{10}$	$\frac{1}{10}$	$\frac{1}{10}$	$\frac{1}{10}$

Complete the equivalent fraction pairs.

1. $\frac{3}{6} = \frac{1}{\square}$

2. $\frac{3}{4} = \frac{\square}{8}$

3. $\frac{1}{5} = \frac{\square}{10}$

4. $\frac{\square}{4} = \frac{2}{8}$

5. $\frac{2}{6} = \frac{1}{\square}$

6. $\frac{4}{\square} = \frac{8}{10}$

7. $\frac{4}{6} = \frac{\square}{3}$

8. $\frac{4}{8} = \frac{\square}{6}$

Simplify these fractions.

9. $\frac{6}{8}$

10. $\frac{2}{4}$

11. $\frac{4}{10}$

12. $\frac{2}{6}$

13. $\frac{3}{6}$

14. $\frac{8}{10}$

15. $\frac{2}{8}$

16. $\frac{6}{10}$

I am confident with finding equivalent fractions and simplifying fractions.

Complete the equivalent fraction pairs.

1. $\frac{6}{9} = \frac{2}{\square}$

2. $\frac{3}{12} = \frac{\square}{4}$

3. $\frac{4}{5} = \frac{\square}{10}$

4. $\frac{\square}{4} = \frac{9}{12}$

5. $\frac{15}{20} = \frac{3}{\square}$

6. $\frac{2}{\square} = \frac{8}{20}$

7. $\frac{2}{3} = \frac{\square}{15}$

8. $\frac{8}{12} = \frac{\square}{3}$

Simplify these fractions.

9. $\frac{6}{15}$

10. $\frac{3}{18}$

11. $\frac{6}{14}$

12. $\frac{14}{21}$

13. $\frac{5}{20}$ $\frac{10}{20}$ $\frac{15}{20}$

> Can the top and bottom number be divided by the same number?

14. $\frac{2}{16}$ $\frac{4}{16}$ $\frac{8}{16}$ $\frac{12}{16}$

15. $\frac{2}{24}$ $\frac{3}{24}$ $\frac{4}{24}$ $\frac{6}{24}$ $\frac{8}{24}$ $\frac{12}{24}$

 **THINK** Is it possible to have a fraction equivalent to $\frac{1}{4}$ that has an odd denominator?

I am confident with finding equivalent fractions and simplifying fractions.

Decimals

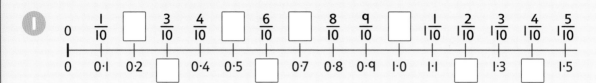
Write the missing fractions and decimals.

1

0 — $\frac{1}{10}$ — ☐ — $\frac{3}{10}$ — $\frac{4}{10}$ — ☐ — $\frac{6}{10}$ — ☐ — $\frac{8}{10}$ — $\frac{9}{10}$ — ☐ — $1\frac{1}{10}$ — $1\frac{2}{10}$ — $1\frac{3}{10}$ — $1\frac{4}{10}$ — $1\frac{5}{10}$

0 — 0·1 — 0·2 — ☐ — 0·4 — 0·5 — ☐ — 0·7 — 0·8 — 0·9 — 1·0 — 1·1 — ☐ — 1·3 — ☐ — 1·5

2

0 — $\frac{1}{10}$ — $\frac{2}{10}$ — $\frac{3}{10}$ — ☐ — $\frac{5}{10}$ — $\frac{6}{10}$ — $\frac{7}{10}$ — ☐ — $\frac{9}{10}$ — $\frac{10}{10}$ — $1\frac{1}{10}$ — 1 ☐ — $1\frac{3}{10}$ — $1\frac{4}{10}$ — 1 ☐

0 — ☐ — 0·2 — 0·3 — 0·4 — ☐ — 0·6 — ☐ — 0·8 — 0·9 — 1·0 — ☐ — 1·2 — 1·3 — 1·4 — 1·5

3

$\frac{5}{10}$ — $\frac{6}{10}$ — $\frac{7}{10}$ — $\frac{8}{10}$ — ☐ — $\frac{10}{10}$ — $1\frac{1}{10}$ — $1\frac{2}{10}$ — 1 ☐ — $1\frac{4}{10}$ — $1\frac{5}{10}$ — 1 ☐ — $1\frac{7}{10}$ — $1\frac{8}{10}$ — 1 ☐ — $1\frac{10}{10}$

0·5 — 0·6 — ☐ — 0·8 — 0·9 — 1·0 — ☐ — 1·2 — 1·3 — ☐ — 1·5 — 1·6 — 1·7 — ☐ — 1·9 — 2·0

Solve these divisions.

10s	1s	0·1s
5	4	
	3	4

4 34 ÷ 10 = ☐

5 56 ÷ 10 = ☐

6 4·2 × 10 = ☐

7 85 ÷ 10 = ☐

8 1·3 × 10 = ☐

9 5·6 × 10 = ☐

10 44 ÷ 10 = ☐

11 8·1 × 10 = ☐

12 99 ÷ 10 = ☐

○ **I am confident with tenths as fractions and decimals.**
○
○

57

Write each decimal as a fraction.

1 0·7

4 0·6

2 0·2

5 0·9

3 0·8

6 0·3

Write each fraction as a decimal.

7 $\frac{4}{10}$

10 $\frac{7}{10}$

8 $\frac{9}{10}$

11 $\frac{5}{10}$ or $\frac{1}{2}$

9 $\frac{1}{10}$

12 $\frac{2}{10}$ or $\frac{1}{5}$

Copy each line and write the box numbers.

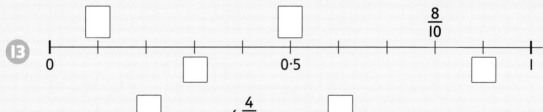

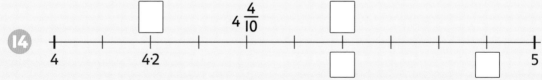

Answer these questions.

15 $\boxed{} \times 10 = 34$

17 $\boxed{} \div 10 = 4·2$

16 $\boxed{} \div 10 = 5·5$

18 $\boxed{} \times 10 = 29$

○
○ **I am confident with tenths as fractions and decimals.**
○

Write each decimal as a fraction and then mark them on a number line.

1 0·2

3 1·1

5 2·7

2 0·6

4 1·4

6 4·8

Write each fraction as a decimal. Write them in order, smallest to largest.

7 $1\frac{4}{10}$

9 $2\frac{6}{10}$

11 $2\frac{3}{10}$

8 $2\frac{1}{10}$

10 $1\frac{9}{10}$

12 $1\frac{1}{2}$ or $1\frac{5}{10}$

Copy this place value grid and write the answers to these questions on it.

100s	10s	1s	0·1s

13 2·2 × 10 = ☐

16 0·7 × 10 = ☐

14 31 ÷ 10 = ☐

17 140 ÷ 10 = ☐

15 53·8 × 10 = ☐

18 111 ÷ 10 = ☐

I am confident with writing and ordering tenths as fractions and decimals.

Adding 4-digit numbers

Choose either the expanded or compact method of addition to answer these.

$3482 + 1464 =$

3000	400	80	2
+ 1000	400	60	4
4000	800	140	6	= 4946

```
  3482
+ 1464
     1
  4946
```

1. 3181
    + 2445

2. 2317
    + 1635

3. 4363
    + 2835

4. 2282
    + 4474

5. 5534
    + 2745

6. 6641
    + 1635

7. 4833
    + 4119

8. 5606
    + 3265

9. 6373
    + 1473

10. 5082
    + 3075

11. 7844
    + 1127

12. 5158
    + 3633

THINK

Answer these and explain what patterns you notice.

1234	2345	3456	4567
+ 4321	+ 5432	+ 6543	+ 7654

Be careful on the last one!

○○○ **I am confident with adding two 4-digit numbers.**

Solve these additions.

1 3573 + 4377 = ☐

2 1608 + 2602 = ☐

3 2257 + 7458 = ☐

4 1547 + 5353 = ☐

5 2398 + 4475 = ☐

6 2451 + 5674 + 17 = ☐

7 2648 + 1324 = ☐

8 5374 + 1436 = ☐

9 2754 + 356 = ☐

10 2946 + 1161 = ☐

11 4567 + 833 + 271 = ☐

12 1047 + 6283 + 22 = ☐

This table shows a code where each letter stands for a digit.

a	b	c	d	e	f	g	h	i	j
0	1	2	3	4	5	6	7	8	9

What are the answers to these additions as numbers?

13 bead + face

14 feed + cage

15 hide + edge + dig

16 Jade + Jed + Gabe + Ed

THINK Write an addition of two 3-digit numbers with a total of 1000 where you have to exchange a 10 and a 100.

○
○ **I am confident with adding two 4-digit numbers.**
○

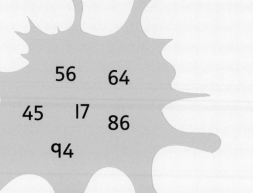

56   64

45   17   86

94

4753

2648   2517

9632   8593

4622

752   185   391

593   808   362

1. What is the smallest answer you can make?

2. What is the largest answer you can make?

3. What is the closest answer to 5000 you can make?

4. What is the closest answer to 9000 you can make?

Use column addition to answer these.

5. Choose two numbers from the purple splat and add them.

6. Choose three numbers from the orange splat and add them.

I am confident with column addition of numbers with up to 4 digits.

1   4673
+ 2465
_____

5   5884
+ 3645
_____

9   7923
+ 4145
_____

2   8437
+ 3535
_____

6   6641
+ 7632
_____

10   5082
+ 3975
_____

3   5188
+ 4835
_____

7   4807
+ 2319
_____

11   7444
+ 2823
_____

4   6482
+ 3975
_____

8   5608
+ 3975
_____

12   5068
+ 1837
_____

13 Jo has two bank accounts. In one there is £6411 and in the other there is £2389. How much has Jo in total?

 Answer these and explain what patterns you notice.

4567   4567   4567   4567   4567
+ 5432   + 6543   + 7654   + 8765   + 9876
_____   _____   _____   _____   _____

I am confident with column addition up of numbers with up to 4 digits.

 **THINK** Which of these additions do you think will give the largest answer? Which do you think will give the smallest answer?

① 6812
\+ 5256
———

⑤ 5787
\+ 8145
———

⑨ 7923
\+ 3697
———

② 6193
\+ 2864
———

⑥ 6829
\+ 4535
———

⑩ 6947
\+ 5975
———

③ 6333
\+ 3934
———

⑦ 4887
\+ 2359
———

⑪ 7485
\+ 5819
———

④ 6179
\+ 1726
———

⑧ 5698
\+ 2309
———

⑫ 5608
\+ 8977
———

⑬ Write a 4-digit addition question with the answer 11 053.

Weight in grams and kilograms

Write the most likely weight of each creature.

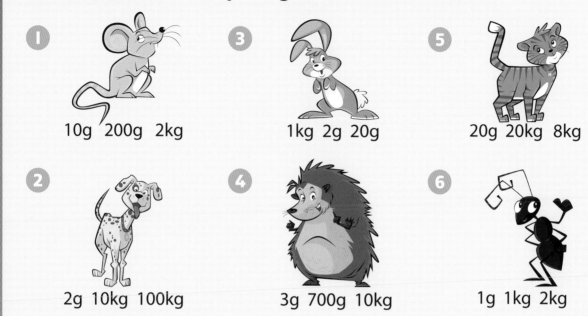

1 10g 200g 2kg

3 1kg 2g 20g

5 20g 20kg 8kg

2 2g 10kg 100kg

4 3g 700g 10kg

6 1g 1kg 2kg

Write each amount in kilograms.

7 1250 g . . .

9 1000 g . . .

11 500 g . . .

13 2500 g . . .

8 2000 g . . .

10 750 g . . .

12 1500 g . . .

14 2750 g . . .

THINK Think of an animal. Discuss with your partner what unit you would use to weigh it. Repeat this for a different animal.

○
○ **I am confident with choosing appropriate units of**
○ **weight and converting between grams and kilograms.**

Write each weight in grams and then kilograms.

 1

3

5

2

4

6

True or false?

7 1 kg is more than 500 g.

8 Two $\frac{1}{2}$ kg bags of coal are heavier than a 1 kg bag of cotton wool.

9 Five 200 g weights are the same as 1 kg.

10 $1\frac{3}{4}$ kg is the same as 1750 g.

11 Three $\frac{1}{2}$ kg packets of flour weigh exactly 1600 g.

12 A hamster could weigh 50 kg.

THINK Write your own statement about weight. Ask your partner if it is true or false.

I am confident with converting between grams and kilograms.

Using bar graphs

The graphs below show the number of different coloured sweets in two large tubes of sweets.

For tube A write how many more sweets are:

1. red than pink

2. blue than yellow

3. orange than red

4. orange than blue

5. yellow than pink.

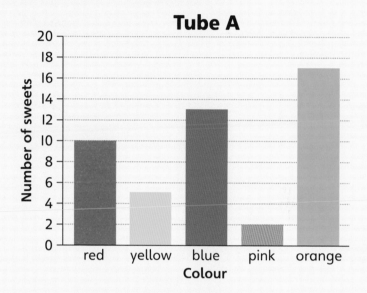

For tube B write how many more sweets are:

6. blue than yellow

7. orange than pink

8. blue than red

9. red than yellow

10. blue than orange.

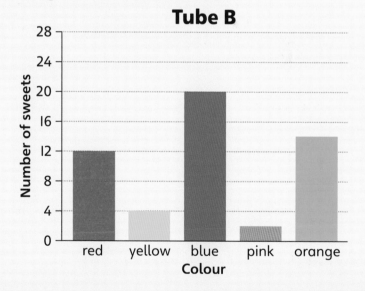

 THINK Which tube held more sweets altogether?

○
○ **I am confident with interpreting information given**
○ **in bar graphs.**

67

Answer the questions about each bar graph.

1. Which team scored fewest goals?

2. How many more goals did Southlea score than Windhill?

3. Which team scored 12 more goals than Trinity?

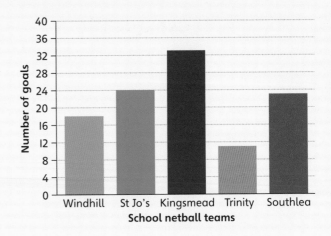

4. How many fewer goals did St Jo's score than Kingsmead?

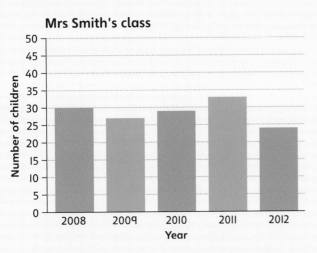

Mrs Smith's class

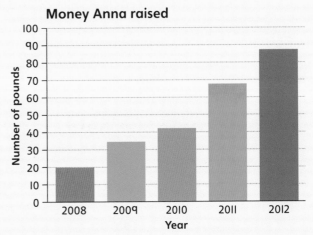

Money Anna raised

How many more children did Mrs Smith have in her class:

5. in 2008 than 2012?

6. in 2011 than 2009?

7. in 2010 than 2009?

8. In which year did she have 5 more children than she had in 2012?

How much did Anna raise in:

9. 2009?

10. 2010?

11. 2012?

12. How much more did she raise in 2011 than in 2008?

13. How much did she raise altogether?

○ **I am confident with interpreting information given**
○
○ **in bar graphs.**

Capacity in litres and millilitres

Answer these questions.

a 250 ml

b 100 ml

c 1200 ml

d 1l

e 1500 ml

f $\frac{3}{4}$ l

g 500 ml

h 600 ml

1. List the containers above that hold less than 1 litre and write how much they contain in litres.

2. List the containers above that hold less than half a litre.

Which container holds less?

3. 450 ml — $\frac{1}{2}$ l

5. $\frac{1}{4}$ l — 200 ml

7. 1l — 600 ml

4. $\frac{3}{4}$ l — 700 ml

6. 850 ml — 1l

8. $\frac{1}{2}$ l — 550 ml

 **THINK** How many 200 ml bottles of water contain the same amount as four $\frac{1}{4}$ l bottles?

○
○ **I am confident with comparing litre and millilitre capacities.**
○

Write each amount using a different unit.

1. 0·4 l = ☐ ml

2. 600 ml = ☐ l

3. 0·7 l = ☐ ml

4. 500 ml = ☐ l

5. 3 l = ☐ ml

6. 2000 l = ☐ l

7. 0·8 l = ☐ ml

8. 900 ml = ☐ l

9. 2300 ml = ☐ l

10. 3·9 l = ☐ ml

11. 1100 ml = ☐ l

12. 2·7 l = ☐ ml

Solve these problems.

13. One shampoo bottle contains 400 ml and another contains 0·3 l. Which holds more and by how much?

14. Sam puts 0·6 l of juice and 200 ml of water into a jug. How many millilitres of drink is in the jug now?

15. A cola bottle holds 800 ml. Roo drinks 0·4 l of it before lunch and 200 ml after lunch. How much does she have left?

I am confident with comparing litre and millilitre capacities.

Write how much is in each container using the unit shown on it.

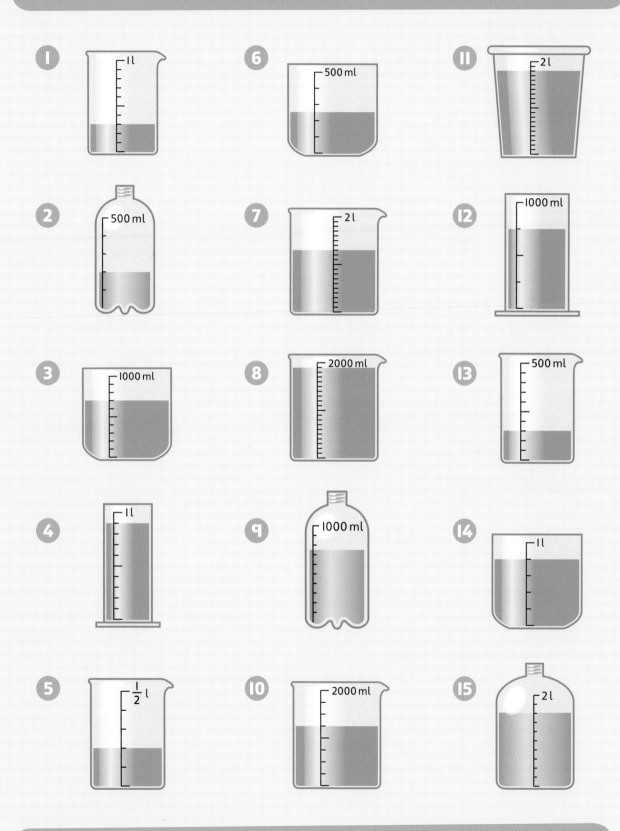

1. 1l
2. 500 ml
3. 1000 ml
4. 1l
5. $\frac{1}{2}$ l

6. 500 ml
7. 2l
8. 2000 ml
9. 1000 ml
10. 2000 ml

11. 2l
12. 1000 ml
13. 500 ml
14. 1l
15. 2l

I am confident with reading and recording litre and millilitre capacities.

1 Match pairs of containers with the same amount of liquid.

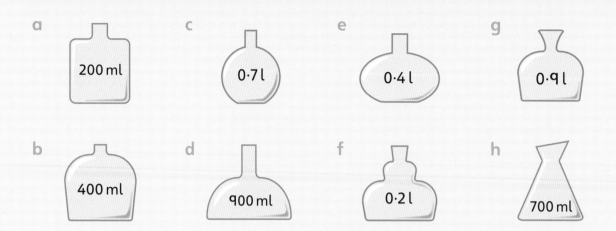

a 200 ml

c 0·7 l

e 0·4 l

g 0·9 l

b 400 ml

d 900 ml

f 0·2 l

h 700 ml

Solve these capacity problems.

2 Carl drinks five 200 ml cups of tea a day. How many litres is this?

3 Mel makes a cocktail using 0·5 l of orange juice, 0·2 l of blackcurrant and 1300 ml of pineapple juice. How many litres of cocktail does she make?

4 400 ml of orange juice is poured into a jug, then 0·8 l of spring water is added. How many millilitres altogether?

5 Jamal has 2 litres of water in a bottle. He drinks 400 ml and spills 0·9 l of it. How many millilitres does he have now?

6 How many 0·2 l cupfuls of water make 3 litres?

THINK Put these in order, starting with the smallest.
400 ml   0·2 l   20 l   1000 ml   0·8 l

1. A bottle contains 200 ml of shampoo. Beth uses 5 ml for each hair wash. How long will the bottle last if she washes her hair every day? How much longer would it last if she used 4 ml every day?

2. Dad fills a 100 l paddling pool with water using a 1250 ml jug. How many times will he need to fill the jug?

3. Amit uses 1500 ml of water to wash his dog. He does this once a month. How many litres does he use in one year?

4. How many 5 ml medicine spoonfuls can you get from a $1\frac{1}{4}$ l bottle of cough mixture?

5. **Match pairs of containers with the same amount of liquid.**

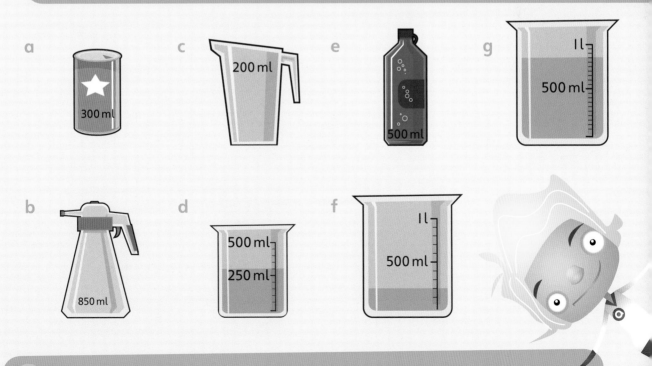

a 300 ml

c 200 ml

e 500 ml

g 1 l 500 ml

b 850 ml

d 500 ml 250 ml

f 1 l 500 ml

I am confident with reading and comparing litre and millilitre capacities.

73

Rounding 4-digit numbers

Round these to the nearest 10.

1

2

3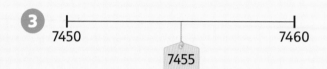

4 1287

5 6844

6 8304

Round these to the nearest 100.

7

8 4578

9 2845

10 5885

Round these to the nearest 1000.

11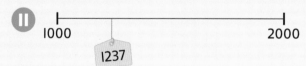

12 4578

13 5145

14 1885

THINK Write a number which rounds to 5000 to the nearest 1000, 4500 to the nearest 100 and 4520 to the nearest 10.

I am confident with rounding 4-digit numbers.

Round each number to the nearest 10, 100 and 1000.

1. 1287
2. 3623
3. 2535
4. 6729
5. 4572

6. 4302
7. 3608
8. 5937
9. 6851
10. 7777

11. 9440
12. 5781
13. 3514
14. 8535
15. 8448

Write a number to match each description.

16. It rounds to 2570 to the nearest 10.

17. It rounds to 8300 to the nearest 100.

18. It is less than 3600 but rounds to 4000 when rounded to the nearest 1000.

19. It rounds to 4000 to the nearest 1000 and to 3500 to the nearest 100.

20. It rounds to 3500 to the nearest 100 and to 3000 to the nearest 1000.

I am confident with rounding 4-digit numbers.

Subtracting 3-digit numbers

GRAB! **Base 10 equipment**

Use this method to answer the subtractions.

$438 - 276 =$

	300	130			
	~~400~~	~~30~~	8		
−	200	70	6		
	1 00	60	2	=	162

1 $673 - 348 =$

		60	13		
	600	~~70~~	~~3~~		
−	300	40	8		
	300	20	5	=	☐

2 $781 - 577 =$

		70	11		
	700	~~80~~	~~1~~		
−	500	70	7		
				=	☐

3 $456 - 391 = ☐$

4 $537 - 318 = ☐$

5 $764 - 527 = ☐$

6 $638 - 276 = ☐$

7 $850 - 527 = ☐$

8 $914 - 751 = ☐$

○
○ **I am confident with subtracting 3-digit numbers**
○ **using the expanded method.**

$426 - 268 =$

```
        110
  300   1̶0̶   16
  4̶0̶0̶   2̶0̶   6̶
- 200   60   8
  100   50   8   =  158
```

1
```
  721
- 392
```

5
```
  436
- 269
```

9
```
  770
- 194
```

2
```
  932
- 283
```

6
```
  554
- 377
```

10
```
  863
- 667
```

3
```
  914
- 565
```

7
```
  376
- 293
```

11
```
  670
- 485
```

4
```
  569
- 381
```

8
```
  881
- 587
```

THINK Choose two subtractions and check your answers using addition.

1) 827
  − 569
  ――

5) 870
  − 565
  ――

9) 646
  − 384
  ――

2) 922
  − 465
  ――

6) 813
  − 687
  ――

10) 563
  − 268
  ――

3) 817
  − 398
  ――

7) 985
  − 447
  ――

11) 880
  − 769
  ――

4) 775
  − 379
  ――

8) 673
  − 277
  ――

12) 715
  − 287
  ――

13) The Empire State Building is 381 m tall. The 21st Century Tower in Dubai is 269 m tall. How much taller is the Empire State Building?

14) The world's tallest man was 272 cm tall. How much taller was he than Jamie, who is 187 cm tall?

15) A block of cheese weighs 723 g. Dan cuts off a chunk weighing 387 g and eats it. How much cheese remains?

 **THINK** Write a column subtraction where the answer has a 9 in the 10s column.

I am confident with column subtraction of 3-digit numbers using the expanded method.

Complete the subtraction to match the jotting.
Use similar jottings to answer the rest.

GRAB! Landmarked number lines

1 800 − 587 = ☐

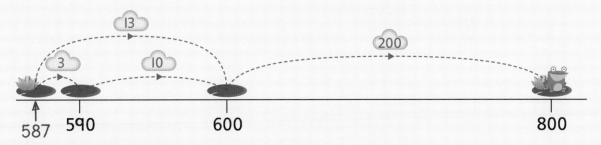

2 701 − 276 = ☐

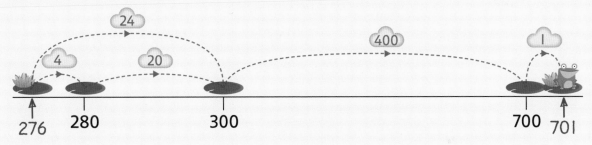

3 400 − 268 = ☐

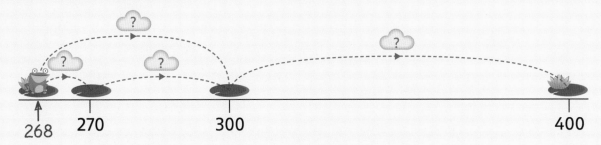

4 600 − 481 = ☐

5 801 − 684 = ☐

6 900 − 569 = ☐

7 602 − 377 = ☐

8 1000 − 785 = ☐

9 1000 − 479 = ☐

I am confident with subtracting 3-digit numbers by counting up.

Use the methods shown to answer these subtractions.

Count up	Column subtraction
1 605 – 486	**6** 486 – 235
2 300 – 184	**7** 538 – 382
3 1002 – 794	**8** 718 – 466
4 3000 – 983	**9** 852 – 437
5 2000 – 1599	**10** 625 – 388

Choose how best to work these out. You could use Frog to count up or column subtraction.

11 800 – 689

14 728 – 589

12 839 – 693

15 1000 – 867

13 404 – 257

16 805 – 682

I am confident with subtracting 3-digit numbers by counting up and using column subtraction.

You could use Frog to count up or column subtraction.

1. 700 – 378

2. 620 – 437

3. 678 – 234

4. 462 – 238

5. 901 – 777

6. 828 – 117

7. 571 – 248

8. 706 – 548

9. 729 – 583

10. 592 – 359

11. 907 – 753

12. 608 – 472

13. 867 – 549

14. 727 – 385

15. 510 – 364

16. 797 – 588

 THINK

Choose two of your answers.
Check each of them using addition.

I am confident with subtracting 3-digit numbers by counting up and using column subtraction.

1. 707 – 378

2. 825 – 637

3. 462 – 278

4. 910 – 674

5. 823 – 237

6. 658 – 259

7. 571 – 288

8. 709 – 523

9. 925 – 783

10. 566 – 289

11. 718 – 402

12. 890 – 449

13. 729 – 458

14. 976 – 757

15. 1010 – 864

16. 2007 – 1599

THINK Choose three of your answers.
Check each of them using addition.

I am confident with subtracting 3-digit numbers by counting up and using column subtraction.

Multiplication using the grid method

Use the method shown to multiply the numbers.

1 4 × 154 = ☐

×	100	50	4
4	400	200	16

= ☐

2 3 × 225 = ☐

3 5 × 132 = ☐

4 415 × 4 = ☐

5 5 × 543 = ☐

6 537 × 3 = ☐

7 5 × 316 = ☐

8 3 × 492 = ☐

9 215 × 8 = ☐

10 7 × 521 = ☐

11 5 × 653 = ☐

Solve these word problems using the same method.

12 A factory makes 341 televisions each day from Monday to Friday. The factory is closed at the weekends. How many televisions does it make each week?

13 How many legs do 256 sheep have?

I am confident with multiplying 3-digit numbers by 1-digit numbers using the grid method.

Use the grid method to multiply the numbers.

1. 6 × 354 = ☐

2. 8 × 526 = ☐

3. 3 × 678 = ☐

4. 467 × 5 = ☐

5. 6 × 589 = ☐

6. 8 × 938 = ☐

7. 7 × 946 = ☐

8. 9 × 578 = ☐

9. 758 × 7 = ☐

10. 9 × 589 = ☐

Solve these word problems.

11. A car manufacturer is making 236 cars. How many wheels are needed?

12. Mrs Hatfield has used her mobile phone to make calls for 342 minutes this month. She will be charged 7p per minute. How much will she be charged for her calls?

 Copy and complete this grid method calculation.

×				
	4800	420	12	=

Multiply these numbers using the grid method.

1 4 × 113 = ☐

×	100	10	3
4	400	40	12

= ☐

2 3 × 231 = ☐

×	200	30	1
3			

= ☐

3 5 × 137 = ☐

×			7
5			

= ☐

4 3 × 451 = ☐

×			

= ☐

5 5 × 543 = ☐

6 4 × 521 = ☐

For these, estimate the answer first before multiplying.

7 3 × 384 = ☐

9 4 × 703 = ☐

8 5 × 613 = ☐

10 3 × 645 = ☐

 **THINK** Write a 3-digit × 1-digit multiplication of your own with an answer between 500 and 1000.

I am confident with multiplying 3-digit numbers by 1-digit numbers using the grid method.

Multiply the numbers, estimating first.

1. $7 \times 573 = \square$

2. $877 \times 9 = \square$

3. $6 \times 964 = \square$

4. $508 \times 7 = \square$

5. $8 \times 859 = \square$

6. $946 \times 6 = \square$

7. $9 \times 538 = \square$

8. $747 \times 7 = \square$

Answer both multiplications in each pair and compare them.

9. Which is greater? 4×378 or 3×478

10. Which is lighter? $5 \times 623\,g$ or $6 \times 523\,g$

11. Which is shorter? $7 \times 661\,cm$ or $6 \times 771\,cm$

12. Which is more? $8 \times £907$ or $9 \times £807$

 **THINK** What could the multiplication below be?

	800	80	4
$\square$	$\square$	$\square$	$\square$

I am confident with multiplying 3-digit numbers by 1-digit numbers using the grid method.

Dividing 2-digit numbers

Divide these numbers using jottings like these.

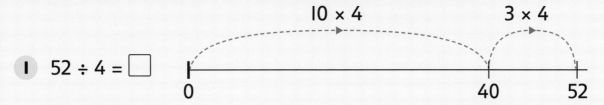

10 × 4   3 × 4

1   52 ÷ 4 = ☐

0   40   52

☐ × 4 = 52
10 × 4 = 40
_____
     12
3 × 4 = 12
_____
      0

13

52 ÷ 4 = ☐

2   84 ÷ 6 = ☐   ☐ × 6 = 84
                        ☐ × 6 = ☐
                        _____
                             ☐
                        ☐ × 6 = ☐
                        _____
                             ☐
        ☐

84 ÷ 6 = ☐

3   48 ÷ 3 = ☐   **6**   76 ÷ 4 = ☐

4   68 ÷ 4 = ☐   **7**   78 ÷ 6 = ☐

5   85 ÷ 5 = ☐   **8**   91 ÷ 7 = ☐

 **THINK**   Which has the larger answer?
98 ÷ 7 or 96 ÷ 6

● I am confident with dividing 2-digit numbers by
● 1-digit numbers with no remainders.

Divide these numbers using jottings like this.

1 $92 \div 4 = \square$ $\square \times 4 = 92$ $92 \div 4 = \square$
$\square \times 4 = \square$
$\square$
$\square \times 4 = \square$
$\square$
$\square$

2 $69 \div 3 = \square$

3 $84 \div 4 = \square$

4 $81 \div 3 = \square$

5 $87 \div 3 = \square$

6 $96 \div 4 = \square$

7 $78 \div 3 = \square$

8 $88 \div 4 = \square$

9 $84 \div 3 = \square$

Solve these problems.

10 Mr Carlos shared £72 between his three children. How much did each child get?

11 Kim had a piece of ribbon 93 cm long. She cut it into three equal lengths. How long was each length?

I am confident with dividing 2-digit numbers by 1-digit numbers with no remainders.

Answer these divisions.

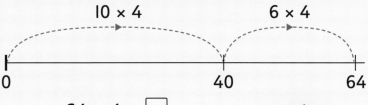

10 × 4   6 × 4

0   40   64

1 64 ÷ 4 = ☐

☐ × 4 = 64
☐ × 4 = ☐
        ☐
☐ × 4 = ☐
        ☐
☐

64 ÷ 4 = ☐

2 78 ÷ 6 = ☐   **4** 76 ÷ 4 = ☐

3 54 ÷ 3 = ☐   **5** 96 ÷ 6 = ☐

Divide these numbers, giving a remainder in each answer.

10 × 3   7 × 3   ?

0   30   51 53

6 53 ÷ 3 = ☐ r ☐

☐ × 3 = 53
☐ × 3 = ☐
        ☐
☐ × 3 = ☐
        ☐
☐

53 ÷ 3 = ☐ r ☐

7 99 ÷ 6 = ☐   **9** 86 ÷ 6 = ☐

8 69 ÷ 4 = ☐   **10** 77 ÷ 4 = ☐

● I am confident with dividing 2-digit numbers by
● 1-digit numbers with and without remainders.

89

1 $55 \div 4 = \boxed{} \, r \, \boxed{}$

$\boxed{} \times 4 = 55$
$\boxed{} \times 4 = \boxed{}$
$\overline{}$
$\boxed{}$
$\boxed{} \times 4 = \boxed{}$
$\boxed{}$
$\boxed{}$

$55 \div 4 = \boxed{} \, r \, \boxed{}$

2 $82 \div 6 = \boxed{} \, r \, \boxed{}$

3 $85 \div 3 = \boxed{} \, r \, \boxed{}$

4 $75 \div 4 = \boxed{} \, r \, \boxed{}$

5 $89 \div 6 = \boxed{} \, r \, \boxed{}$

6 $88 \div 5 = \boxed{} \, r \, \boxed{}$

7 $97 \div 5 = \boxed{} \, r \, \boxed{}$

8 $93 \div 4 = \boxed{} \, r \, \boxed{}$

9 $97 \div 6 = \boxed{} \, r \, \boxed{}$

10 Mrs Jones has 47 biscuits. She shares as many of them out as she can onto three plates so that there is an equal number on each plate. How many biscuits are on each plate? How many are left over?

11 Fred has 94 pound coins. He makes six equal piles of coins as high as he can. How many coins does he have left over?

Answer these divisions.

1 $93 \div 8 = \square$

2 $56 \div 3 = \square$

3 $88 \div 5 = \square$

4 $87 \div 6 = \square$

5 $65 \div 4 = \square$

6 $86 \div 7 = \square$

7 $79 \div 6 = \square$

8 $79 \div 4 = \square$

9 $71 \div 3 = \square$

10 $90 \div 6 = \square$

11 $98 \div 8 = \square$

12 $97 \div 7 = \square$

13 $89 \div 3 = \square$

14 $99 \div 7 = \square$

 **THINK**
Four children eat dinner with 22 fish fingers to be shared equally between them. How many fish fingers will they each have if all of the fish fingers are to be eaten?

I am confident with dividing 2-digit numbers by 1-digit numbers with and without remainders.

Practising calculations

1. $632 - \boxed{} = 600$

2. $723 - 687 = \boxed{}$

3. $\boxed{} \times 6 = 30$

4. $134 - 23 = \boxed{}$

5. $67 \times 2 = \boxed{}$

6. $6 \times 22 = \boxed{}$

7. $14 \times 9 = \boxed{}$

8. $\frac{1}{5}$ of $35 = \boxed{}$

9.
$$817$$
$$336$$
$$+\ 327$$

10.
$$803$$
$$-\ 662$$

11. $481 + \boxed{} = 500$

12. $867 - 549 = \boxed{}$

13. $\boxed{} \div 6 = 8$

14. $175 - 89 = \boxed{}$

15. $901 - 777 = \boxed{}$

16. $521 \times 8 = \boxed{}$

17. $8 \times 77 = \boxed{}$

18. $\frac{1}{9}$ of $99 = \boxed{}$

19. Double 926 is $\boxed{}$

20. $867 - 549 = \boxed{}$

21.
$$6482$$
$$+\ 4274$$

22. Mo has two bank accounts. In one there is £4673 and in the other there is £6383. How much has Mo in total?

23. Jim must drive 600 miles to Glasgow. By 5 o'clock he has driven 527 miles. How much further has he to go?

24. In a sale a TV that cost £400 is reduced by £84. How much does it cost now?

25. How many legs do 345 sheep have?

1. $67 \times 2 = \square$

2. $7 \times 22 = \square$

3. $16 \times 9 = \square$

4. $\frac{1}{10}$ of $60 = \square$

5. $\square \times 6 = 36$

6. $256 - 23 = \square$

7. $846 - \square = 800$

8. $621 - 589 = \square$

9. $\begin{array}{r} 903 \\ - 771 \\ \hline \end{array}$

10. $\begin{array}{r} 374 \\ 271 \\ + 483 \\ \hline \end{array}$

11. $801 - 666 = \square$

12. $421 \times 8 = \square$

13. $9 \times 77 = \square$

14. $\frac{1}{8}$ of $72 = \square$

15. $\square \div 8 = 8$

16. $164 - 87 = \square$

17. $463 + \square = 500$

18. $758 - 549 = \square$

19. $\begin{array}{r} 5738 \\ + 3255 \\ \hline \end{array}$

20. Double 847 is $\square$

21. $567 - 438 = \square$

22. Kim gets £6 each week for pocket money. After how many weeks will she have £72?

23. How many legs do 536 horses have?

24. A factory makes 432 televisions each day from Monday to Friday. The factory is closed at the weekends. How many televisions does it make each week?

25. Dina drives from home to York and back. The total distance driven was 326 km. How far from York is her home?

Tile puzzles

This triangular tile has three numbers.

The numbers can be used to write four multiplication and division facts:

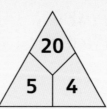

$20 \div 5 = 4$
$20 \div 4 = 5$
$5 \times 4 = 20$
$4 \times 5 = 20$

Write four facts for each of these tiles.

1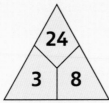

3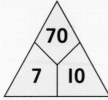

5

2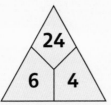

4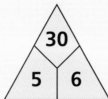

6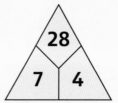

7 Draw some of your own tiles. Make sure the numbers work as correct multiplications and divisions. Can you include a 6 and a 9 in at least two of your tiles?

Which number is missing from each of these?

8

10

12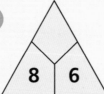

14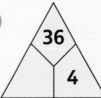

9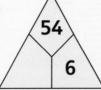

11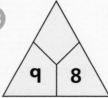

13

15

Spotting patterns

Investigate these different adding and subtracting puzzles. What do you notice?

Puzzle 1

Choose a number between 50 and 100.	75
Reverse the digits.	57
Add the numbers.	75 + 57 = 132
Reverse the digits of your answer.	231
Add the two last numbers	132 + 231 = 363
Is the answer palindromic?	

Palindromic means it is the same if written in reverse!

Puzzle 2

Choose a 3-digit number.	542
Reverse the digits.	245
Find the difference.	542 – 245 = 297
Reverse the digits of your answer.	792
Add the two last numbers	297 + 792 = 1089
Do you always get 1089?	

Puzzle 3

An Indian mathematician, Kaprekar, discovered a pattern in 1949: Choose 4 digits. Make the largest and smallest 4-digit numbers possible with them and find the difference. Now do the same with the digits of the answer. Keep going until you reach Kaprekar's number. What is his number?

Series Editor
Ruth Merttens

Author Team
Jennie Kerwin and Hilda Merttens

Published by Pearson Education Limited, Edinburgh Gate, Harlow, Essex, CM20 2JE.

www.pearsonschools.co.uk

Text © Pearson Education Limited 2013
Typeset by Debbie Oatley @ room9design
Original illustrations © Pearson Education Limited 2013
Illustrated by Matthew Buckley, Marek Jagucki, Andrew Painter, Debbie Oatley
Cover design by Pearson Education Limited
Cover illustration and Abacus character artwork by Volker Beisler © Pearson Education Limited
Additional contributions by Hilary Koll and Steve Mills, CME Projects Ltd.

First published 2013

18
10 9 8

British Library Cataloguing in Publication Data
A catalogue record for this book is available from the British Library

ISBN 978 1 408 27850 5

Printed in the UK by Bell and Bain Ltd, Glasgow

Acknowledgements
We would like to thank the staff and pupils at North Kidlington Primary School, Haydon Wick Primary School, Swindon, St Mary's Catholic Primary School, Bodmin, St Andrew's C of E Primary & Nursery School, Sutton-in-Ashfield, Saint James' C of E Primary School, Southampton and Harborne Primary School, Birmingham, for their invaluable help in the development and trialling of this book.

Every effort has been made to contact copyright holders of material reproduced in this book. Any omissions will be rectified in subsequent printings if notice is given to the publishers.